RAMPANT

Poems by
Nancy Lynée Woo

Don't think about all those things you fear. Just be glad to be here.

-FC Kahuna

Eat a lot. Sleep a lot. Brush 'em like crazy.

-The Beach Boys

For Markus

& The Poetry Lab

Acknowledgements

Many thanks to these publications, in which the poems originally appeared in some version or another:
"Snappy Refrigerator Magnet Saying" *Cadence Collective, cadencecollective.net*
"Little Saigon" *CHEAP POP, cheappoplit.com*
"The Catwalk" *The Camel Saloon, thecamelsaloon.blogspot.com*
"What Are You" *Cease, Cows, ceasecows.com*
"Tiny Feet" *Cease, Cows*
"Penny and a Scratcher" *Melancholy Hyperbole, melancholyhyperbole.com*
"Love in the Fourth Paradigm" *The Camel Saloon*
"States of Deprivation: Neurotic" *Cadence Collective*
"10th Floor, Long Beach Pacific Tower: Monday" *Cadence Collective*
"The Relinquish" *Cadence Collective*
"What to Know About INFPs" *The Subterranean Quarterly, stquarterly.com*
"New Mexico Sea" *Artemis Journal 2014*

Special thanks to Sarah Thursday for her help in kicking my butt in the best way possible to bring my first little book to life.

Cover art by Fernando Gallegos. Thank you Fernando!!
Back cover by René Magritte, "The Lost Jockey"

Contents

Snappy Refrigerator Magnet Saying   1

Little Saigon   2

The Catwalk   3

What Are You   4

Tiny Feet   5

Penny and a Scratcher   6

Love in the Fourth Paradigm   7

States of Deprivation: Neurotic   8

10th Floor, Long Beach Pacific Tower: Monday   11

What to Know About INFPs   13

The Modern Intellectual   14

The Relinquish   15

10 Steps To Englightenment After A Shitty Day   17

New Mexico Sea   20

Snappy Refrigerator Magnet Saying

I like my men how I like my
crossed word puzzles:
complex, frustrating and
nongiveupable –

The only love worth having
labyrinthine.

I am no princess hoping on toads;
Give me your ugly, your worst,
your most frightening Minotaur
and a string.

Little Saigon

We were walking down the street, fresh kumquats in hand, one day in her neighborhood of Little Saigon. Biggest Vietnamese ghetto outside of Vietnam, quietly situated across boba shops and Pho 99s, smack dab in the middle of 1999. My best friend and me, walking past dirt yards and Buddha bellies, swinging our little arms and sucking the juice out of tiny, tart things that weren't quite oranges. We had grabbed them from the red envelope cement of her front yard, where strange smells from the kitchen and karaoke with English subtitles belted out from the peeling paint windows. Circling and circling around the block, bored as an Orange County summer, I opened my 9-year old trap to say, "You're weird." And I giggled. We joked like that, all of us, the half Mexican and the fat Japanese one especially. All us Orange County different-colored girls, poking fun at each other before the boys did, before the ads did, criticizing ourselves like our moms did, every flaw pointed out. I said to her this time, "You're funny weird. You joke weird." This was a compliment. "Yeah!" she said. So I kept going, "In fact, everything about you is weird. You look weird. You talk weird. You dance weird. You smell weird!" She was laughing with me until. Quiet. I stopped. We walked. Throwing away the skins now. Passing the house where the dog cried all day long, and then, one day, didn't. "You think I look weird?" Stammer. "No," I said. She cringed at me with long Viet face, big lidless eyes, framed by muddy cream skin and flat tracks of black hair, fallen. "I always thought I looked weird," she said. I stared back, chubby China cheeks and big teeth, fat stupid fists wanting to ball up and kill the guy who killed his dog. We drifted back to her house, then drifted apart after 5th grade. What she didn't realize was, what I didn't say was, what I couldn't say was, I didn't mean it. A mirror can't be offended. We're in this together. Your face is mine.

The Catwalk

The reason why I don't clean
or fix my car, and then drive
around Belmont Shore looking
smug with taillights smashed
and duct tape mirrors gaping
at the fluffed white people
shopping is because I might want
them to be offended by my
poorness. I learned this in
4th grade when I would, without
fail, walk into my Gifted And
Talented Education classroom—
where smart kids go to be told
they're smart—in Orange County—
where the envious go to flourish
in their hive cement sidewalks—
15 minutes late every day, creaking
open the door to teacher already
talking, interrupting, because
my mother, worn out and coffee-fixed,
could never fit a schedule,
it was her subtle way of resisting
her tug-a-long fate—at least she could
rebel against time—and usually
my clothes were dirty or old or
hand-me-downs friends' mothers
who pitied me gave me, and here
I learned how to walk in this rag
fashion show kind of way, quiet but
smiling that smile like I was saying
yeah, look at me, look at the isness
of my difference, I'll strut on in
when I want and grin until
you believe I am grinning, smirk
wide like I am better than you for
knowing what poverty feels like.

What Are You

I hold my nose and fish my sister's friendship ring out of the toilet because, at 9, I sense that we need that kind of thing to face what probably smells like shame. We have the same bone structure. She bites harder than I do, but we are both aliens. Starchildren, if you listen to Mona Jade. Though I don't have any proof other than my eyelids, flat nose, bad teeth. My "What are you?" answers, different every time, depending on which star I'm floating on that day. *What's it to you* when I'm a grump, or *Why don't you take a guess* if I'm feeling flirty. But come on, "What are you?" with that glowy look of a man imagining traveling to China's sewers. I'm from fucking Orange County! I let that one squirm out only when I hate myself and my hair is stringy, mostly. It's such a tiny part of any day to not have enough boxes for what's fully in you. But there are enough labeled specifically "check one" to remind you that you are a pioneer, a checkerboard mystery, a NASA Hubble Cassini Kepler all in one. A hybrid monkey-cat mewing all the way to the Milky Way, making collages out of dust.

Tiny Feet

Gung-man, the father, better known as Bob to everyone else, found out at 50 there was white blood in the family. This was after he was disgraced for marrying my sweet blonde mom. Disowned completely. No big Christmases for mutt babies. No dim sum, no dragon dance, no name in funny sounds. The Chinese don't just not share their secrets. Did you know they don't have any at all. Experts at forgetting, professionals in fact. My heart on Sunday mornings is a colander and my soul southern fried chicken dumplings wanting to be fresh, sacred. That's when, for 20 years, Gung-man didn't smile, only let it bake inside. But also, you know there are tunnels in every room. Like how my grandmother, then my mother, then me, never talked about the other side, how those wisps of children transformed into pebbles in our throats. Still, I was born. I have a feeling I came out tossing and tumbling on the crazy wagon like my grandmother, who said she loved America. 1967 Loving v. Virginia, the landmark Supreme Court case recognizing interracial marriage, does not address Chinese honor. So now when my straight up Anglo friends travel to China and the Chinese are so stoked to see real live white people like in the movies, they buzz around them like they're celebrities. I wonder what it felt like for chee-thlee, the crazy one, to have such tiny feet. Bound up, wrapped in tape for decades until the blood vessels had been trained to obey. I wonder what her face looked like when she found out she had a mongrel for a granddaughter, tiny blood vessels popping as her fury echoed forward in time, all the way through to baby's first birthday, kindergarten graduation, graduations upon graduations, divorces and bad stunts. You know she put a curse on us.

Penny and a Scratcher

I don't know if my parents had
big dreams I don't know if they
fell deeply into young love I don't
know if they ever cried for the
beauty of youth,
all I know is when I see my dad's
listless form slumped in front of
the TV or my mom's empty eyes,
childlike and so pretty with make-
up, I feel an ache for their aging
unhappiness and wonder if
it was ever any different, if apathy
ever looked good on them, if forks
in the road that twine through hearts
and break blood with steel
can ever be forgotten.
"I'm feeling lucky tonight, "
mother says with starbright eyes,
keys jingling to the car from 7-11.
She hands my sister and me a
penny and a scratcher, singing
to the sky out of a lipstick crescent
moon, "I have both of you with me
tonight."

As we scratch away, the eagerness
fades over our yesterday talk
of beginnings and bright futures,
over my parents' yellowing questions
of how did we get to be so old, and
when we don't win anything, she
still smiles sadly, as we drive off into
the polluted haze of another L.A. sunset.

Love in the Fourth Paradigm

1

Open up my dirty puckered lips
safeguarding
tainted paradise
will you please

2

Bruise my ego into air
and let go the fourth dimension's
mysteries, what comes next

3

Will you waltz with me from one overdone love song
in the lower
out to the endless white of the fourth paradigm,
the flower of life cradling
our nakedness in every direction,
spidering us beyond
first world traps

(two souls found don't have to die in each other)

and maybe back

4

out there must be a better name than Love,
our bodies such thin fabric
repeating
diagrams unseen

States of Deprivation: Neurotic

I need to eat something, I need to stop smoking.
I can eat later, I need to cut the excess from my nails,
I need to feed the cat, scrub the tub, check the mail
ten times a day, forget to log failures and remember
why I dove in.
I need to look at pictures of kids with malaria and other
terrible diseases to feel lucky. I need to get off my ass.
I need to feel my feet on the ground. See a beach in my head.
I need love, or to give more, or to stop giving so much.
I need to learn
how to ask for things better, and I suppose trust.
I need to know who to trust. I need to know more things
than adding hot water to ramen. I *could* need
a great death again. My own funeral. I could ask
Where is my phoenix? Maybe I want a child to stare at.
Or a pony to train. I have tofu why don't I cook it.
I need to know what to do.
Today is my day and I am depleted.
I want an analog classroom but a digital studio.
I have too much floor space and not enough
hammers. I need to spend less time on the Internet but
more time on the Internet because I need to understand
things. I need to learn web design, and classical
piano and dance, oh how I need to dance. Also
messy but controlled drawing because
I've got plans. I need to improve
my friendship skills.
Or maybe a cat is enough, purring and
squeaks are enough.
I need water. We all need
water, good clean water, not hard mineral bone-
calcifying water. But aren't we lucky? We have
first world residue, boxed in worlds
away from each other. Our pipes
feeding our cells shared trash.
I need to swim in the polluted lake.

I need to clean it.
I need to catch Lyme disease and then
cure it, I need to understand hunger. I could
not eat for a week. Or I could ravage elephant meat
if I had to. I could rip tender flesh from under a still-
live tortoise shell if I had to. I could never eat
In-N-Out again
if I had to.
I could smoke until my lungs
crumbled or I could not if I had to. I could pretend love
is a ferry I'd travel to the Underworld for and
redemption is music.
And never look back if it suits me.
Or I could gut the fish of need. And wear the bones
around my neck, in between eyeballs,
dancing in the forest, with only my cats if I want to.
350 people die
in Britain every year from crazy cat disease.
Schizophrenic hallucinations transferred
through playful claws, is that already me?
I could love in that feral way. I could push myself to the edge
just to feel it. I could remember my childhood like four
tiny walls and TV dinners pushed through slots and
recreate it.
Or I could balance on a fine point.
Scribble darling nothings into the sea,
having built a raft. Here it is. Waffle and waffle around
for a while. Eat trembling
for dinner and catcall out into the asphalt wilderness
I'm too young! to be weary and too old!
to be dull. I could shine my knives.
I don't have any knives. I could
jump *into* the lake
and see what it feels like to swim
with Loch Ness on its lunch break.
I'm not saying wait but

I could want to live with a
reformed monster with fishtails
for eyes, the kind who knows
what depth tastes like.
Maybe something like that. Maybe
nothing at all like that. Maybe
it doesn't matter, I've got plenty
of mirrors and a funhouse
of voices in my head to keep me
company. But either way, not anybody
too stark or big-mouthed or needy
or conventional. What was I supposed
to be doing again. Risk floating forever.
I could float forever.

10th Floor, Long Beach Pacific Tower: Monday

I am in my office.
Brand new Mac shines gleamingly on the tech stand,
eyes to brain to hand to mouse to cursor.
Organizing words and numbers into
rows and columns:
control C to control Z, new tab control T,
click, command tab to switch windows,
that's when

(after earlier reconciling the left and right hemispheres
—they had overloaded with
caffeine and too many synchronous connections
not to notice,
the heart wondering, the task list beckoning,
neurons buzzing like bees in a jar
so that stars crossed in x's across the horizon of my forehead and
we, my brain and I, had to lie in bed to slow the whirring,
scan the left, scan the right,
find the source and troubleshoot—
putting my mind back into working order like
rejoining two soggy sides of a hamburger bun, smoosh)

suddenly on the 10th floor of the Pacific Tower
right in the middle of full immersion,
(well-oiled left side jackhammering, nailing and blazing
through one nearly complete Excel file,
why then do some memories appear,
right side forcing open the door with jelly-filled balloons
yelling Happy Birthday! when it is nowhere near)

I am suddenly driving my 1997 beat up but air conditioned tank of
a Camry through miles and miles of orchards

on the illustrious San Juan Road,
the best backroad shortcut from here to Santa Cruz, just one long

single lane curving up and around strawberries and blackberries
growing in rows and columns, organizing themselves from some
great design into sweetness

whizzing 300 miles away from the cement of L.A.

wheels spinning forward, I'm not just arriving but cruising
with someone, someone special, could be any of them
any of those sharp soft eyes meeting mine in the passenger's seat
my gaze is forward but I can feel them next to me

and when it's been 5 hours now we start to chart our souls
stretching, bingeing on smart water, snacks, cigarettes, skin
sticking to flimsy shorts and singing, terrible singing!

and when we pass the big red barn, one hour left we celebrate!
the road seems to speed with us, then past the giant billboard of
children, that one fake horse and the restaurant, Casa de Fruta,
where I once bought expensive wines and then let them overheat
to vinegar

the comfort of little markers that tell us we've been here before

and always, music plays loud on the stereo,
some eclectic playlist mixing beats with nostalgia,
soothing us into déjà vu, into exactly
what I am listening to right now

back in the office, half brain humming half brain working
in white desk reverie, dragging & dropping and copying & pasting
and accurately compiling everything we need to know
that is practical and trackable and saveable
into clean little boxes where

in a 10 by 10 pristine network of wires and cables
I realize it's been a while since I've been there,
it's been a while since that long, cozy road
and I remember it is not my job to enjoy
when my computer processor glitches
with memories of new love.

What To Know About INFPs

They carry peace bombs in their foreheads. Ready to explode should you just extend one hand, nay, one pinkie finger to help lighten the load. The bomb builds back up again every night. Their dreams are of colors we can't yet see, and they are quiet builders, master blenders, mantis shrimp. When the whirring starts in the morning, you know someone is throwing all the colored fruits into the mix. Serving it to you like a rainbow juice from the other world, extravagant. Though, when the world is not those beautiful clouds from that beautiful dream, it's the deepest mud-brown from where she faceplants into the waste stream. Some may encourage wrapping those red claws in rubber bands and throwing it all into the boil. She starts to smell herself. That's when the screaming starts. All irrationalities become clearer than wood. Ready to stew. She is rotten, no good. Until. Your pinkie. Extends. And then, boom.

The Modern Intellectual

Look, there you are
     with your high bridled boots
          and your fedora tilting down over
perfectly impartial
     long flowing hair, concentrating
          hard on pushing out
              some great thought,
bent over naked and
     pooping
into a steel-chambered bowl.

The Relinquish

No longer are you the invigorate
or the titillate
of my exalt

I must do the dump of the dishwater
and remove the cherish
from my nightstand

clean out your linger and your sulk,
scrub down your rouse and chafe.

Deep hold of hesitate.

The dreams grow thicker
with my linger
though like every sour savor

I wake with tongue heavy,
pockmarked.

How can I get out from underneath
your elevate?

Haughty sticks around a fire,
I throw it all into the languish.

Is it my mind, my misguided
arteries pumping or my swollen skin
that needs you

to narrate how my cells squirm?
Does my heart exist in my body
or yours?

Underground of the resist, I follow
the ethered string that links us
to the crevice where I keep my agonize –

it is hard and yellow, and
smells of sulfur, a deep recess where
nothing but slime is born,
but I remember.

I remember when I thought
surrender would be a palace.

10 Steps To Enlightenment After A Shitty Day

1. Let go of your eyeballs. It's won't be easy at first, but they're just thick, gooey little planets lodged in a skull made of the dust of time and you're a tinkerer. No big deal. Let 'em go. They'll be there when you return. If you relax hard enough, maybe you'll even catch a glimpse of them in all their tiny, faceted glory. Blue? Brown? Catlike? Snakelike? Shining with a million lights?

2. Work on seeing yourself better than others see you. Hold the marble of your thoughts in your palm, squeeze it and then let it shatter. As you sit there in the blackness with your eyeballs elsewhere, focus all your attention on trying to see the wall behind you. Let me repeat: you are trying to SEE the WALL that is BEHIND you. Practice. Someday, you might get an idea of what it's like to ride your favorite zebra gracefully down the halls of the everything maritime space zoo. Surprisingly, it's quiet and feels like fall.

3. Breathe. Remember this part, but forget anyone telling you what to do, forget all the sweaty smiles and impersonal prescriptions for your anxiety-ridden stress brain when what you really need is a home-cooked meal and something that feels like family. Forget about good intentions and not good enough, and just remember to inhale with intention. Own alone. Forget about New Age, forget about hokey. Do it deeply enough so it can graze the surface of the ache and maybe, later on, enter.

4. Did you know, you don't have to be attached to hating yourself? But if you are, write it all down and read it out loud so you know how ridiculous it sounds. What's wrong with your over-caring and sour tongue words and wretched self-image? Nothing. If you absolutely need some negative sculpture to hang your too many hats on, remember the abyss in the eyes of a man whose gaze you couldn't hold for more than a quarter second without internalizing the terror of that empty, black hole vortex mind, the kind serial killers spiral downwards in. Shudder, and thank yourself for feeling.

5. Let the confusion settle. Wonder if you should finally take the plunge and drag yourself into the waiting room to pick up a generic prescription for that everyday affliction that haunts most of the people you know. You'd like to be more special than antidepressants. You'd like to think you get it, really. That all of this is moving towards something. That even the darkest moments tremble with purpose. But the Himalayas are impractical at this point in your life, and you can't meditate all day in a room you have to shuck out 600 bucks just to sleep in. Serotonin is real. Consider all your options.

6. But don't let your mind mislead you. If you can get rid of your eyeballs, the mind isn't so scary. Sometimes it's the heart, where Nessie the Loch Ness monster of your ribcage thrashes around in whiplash agony at her impertinent prison. It'd be news to me but I don't think they've found a pill to cure heartbreak yet. She'll calm down in time. If your throat starts to swell with bile just imagining, say something like, "Calm down, Nessie. I'll feed you when I can."

7. Be terrified. Be miserable. Be outrageously, horrendously, unabashedly a stinking fuck no one wants to be around, but don't be around them while you purge. It's important to purge, more necessary than confession or believing in sin or fake smiling. Let yourself go there, go there deeply, get familiar with the blank walls, but only go there if you promise not to stay. Let your hell be a bed and breakfast you can't afford to visit all the time. But while you're there and you've got a few ethereal, grandmothery caretakers watching out for you, you might as well let the rot well up from the inside and eat away at your need like acid. Let every cell in your body sizzle like you're being dipped in fire, self-immolating in protest of a regime too totalitarian to live through – oh, this unfair world, oh, this imperfect life, your absent family, your crawling dreams, your crippling self-doubt and panicked fear, your self-proclaimed ugliness, your disappointing job, the meager scraps you call living and especially the guilt – set it all to fire. Scream, cry, yell, stare listlessly, whatever. Let your body heave out the poison of the mind.

8. But – this is important – don't dwell in the furnace or it will eat you alive. Let your misery burn for, say, an hour or two, or until it's enough. Let yourself reach the ends like a traveler on her last breath. Don't dawdle, but you'll get there when you get there. Know when you get there. Then, pull yourself out – this is the hardest part. Do it anyway. Train yourself to do it, and do it faster every time. An Olympic swimmer pummeling through the laps of a toxic swamp, shaving off seconds in victory. Really, this is the part that should get your pulse racing, more exciting than Disneyland because what you have been waiting for is not a fairytale spectacle. It may be just a moment, but a moment that becomes familiar – your suffering transforms into bendable metal you use for letting important things dry. Memos and invoices and collecting your dues from the inside out. A strange calm. You dip a pen in the ash to see what remains. And there, appears the glimmer of movement. How refreshing that you will make new mistakes, and make them better, not bitter.

9. Be totally 100% okay with waiting for something, maybe you don't know what. Know that you will have changed already. And then do something. Tangible. Hang a whiteboard. Write on a whiteboard after you've hung it. Organize your papers or shoes or books. Cut your toenails. Take a shower. Do the dishes. Yodel if that's what comes to you. Start remembering your existence. Make a plan for tomorrow.

10. And when you're ready, pick up those eyeballs from wherever they lay. Dust them off with the dust of all dust. They may not feel any different. They may still feel like bowling ball silly putty. But when you can see the wall behind you with your eyes shut (it's no easier with eyes open), when you have memorized its grooves with unfailing accuracy, when you can recount the details of its origin in perfect detail – once you can see that wall behind you, you will have practiced enough.

You will never, ever practice enough. But you will practice. And you will practice. And you will see.

New Mexico Sea

Hot pueblo roads, adobe brick crashing two
warm bodies into sun, there was no
trace of ocean there. No trace
of vast, seaworn volcanoes
sending ripples up
and out,
only smooth rocks
perfect for touching, for learning
the names of, for grabbing onto their easy material
existence. No threat of deep undercurrents.
There are no riptides in New Mexico
anymore—it's been
500 million years
since any
shallow sea
complicated the foundation, and centuries since
the last Apache chief put down his head
and his pipe one final time—no
there are only
slow
moving
desert tortoises
who survive by knowing when
to turn themselves into perfect shelter, their armory
my currency here, and coyotes who know
how to celebrate
a kill.
So when he grabbed
the easy material existence of me, it was like by a man
incapable of drowning, the dry desert air
impatient
to forget salt.
And I did not fear

for losing myself, I was too far from the Pacific,
reflections in the road just mirages
you don't have to worry about
and lovers only die of
starvation
here.
Luckily,
I was full of eating sand, I had bloated
into a heavyweight version of myself, a contoured
container like sandbags for the dunes
made of wind—separate and
packed tight
to keep
distant waves from pummeling
the face of the shore. I could not be swept away, and so
when the smooth polished stone of his body
skipped over me, finally
I did not feel
I was being
pulled under.

Nancy Lynée Woo has been writing poems since she was 8 years old but is only recently out of denial that she does in fact write poems. (She does in fact write poems!) She is so fortunate to have found a lovely poetry home in Long Beach, CA with the fine folks of the Poetry Lab. She's been a featured reader with Rose Writers of Amherst Writers & Artists, the Poetry Lab and the Pondwater Society.

Before the poetry fire was fully lit, Nancy earned a degree in sociology from UC Santa Cruz, then spent the lost years after college flitting around as a Jane of a million trades, doing freelance writing, editing, tutoring, blogging, reporting, event planning, organizing, and marketing and stuff. Now, she is working full-time as an writer/editor while continuing to write, dance and throw parties, you know? You can follow her on Twitter @fancifulnance.

"Don't ask what the world needs. Ask what makes you come alive, and go do it. Because what the world needs is people who have come alive." -Howard Thurman